D0467755

Design   David West

Editor   Steve Parker

Researcher   Cecilia Weston-Baker

Illustrator   Aziz Khan

Consultant   Michele Verroken
                Sports Development Unit,
                The Sports Council, UK

Designed and produced by
Aladdin Books Ltd
70 Old Compton Street
London W1

First published in the
United States in 1988 by
Franklin Watts
387 Park Avenue South
New York NY 10016

ISBN 0 531 10626 8

Library of Congress Catalog
Card Number: 88 50494

Printed in Belgium

Contents

Introduction   5
Why take sports drugs?   7
Drugs misuse in sports   15
The harm in drugs   29
Drug testing and the rules   37
The trade in sports drugs   47
Winning without drugs   53
Drug profiles   58
Sources of help   60
What the words mean   61
Index   62

UNDERSTANDING DRUGS

DRUGS, STEROIDS AND SPORTS

Janet Mohun

FRANKLIN WATTS
New York · London · Toronto · Sydney

INTRODUCTION

Sports are no longer simply sports. They are also big business. In the old days, winning was the main aim. Today, other rewards for the winner can be enormous, in terms of status, fame, adulation . . . and of course money. As the stakes get higher, competitors continually look for ways to improve their chances of becoming champions – at school, college, and on the national and international level. A few have turned to drugs. They believe that drugs will give them that all-important edge over their opponents.

Drugs are substances intended to treat people who are ill. Taking them in an attempt to do better at sports is usually dangerous, sometimes deadly, and always cheating.

Despite this, drug-taking ("doping" as it is called) has become more and more widespread in the last 20 years. It now seems to affect many sports, from snooker to weightlifting, from gymnastics to archery. Some of the misused drugs are illegal in most countries, and are rarely used in medicine because of their risky side-effects. But others are easier to get hold of, and have lots of genuine medical uses.

The costs to people who dope themselves for sports are high. Even if there are short-term gains, in the end, it's the person who takes the drug who loses. Any drug can be dangerous, especially when taken for a long time and in high doses, as it often is in sports. Used correctly, drugs can

Agony or ecstacy? Emotions spill over at top-level meetings.

save lives. But misused, they can be destroyers of health. Several successful athletes have paid for their desire to win – with their lives.

It's not only your health that you risk if you misuse drugs. Across the world, sport itself is coming down hard on people who think they need drugs to help them win. Takers of banned drugs risk losing their title, their respect, and a ban or suspension from competition. If they are professionals, they lose their livelihood.

Drug misuse also sours the name of good sports. And not only the takers themselves are to blame. The idea of fair competition, where "the best person wins," is dashed by the team-mates, managers and coaches who cover up drug abuse, and by the crooked physicians who supply the drugs.

If you are an aspiring champion or a muscle-pumping teenager, there may come a time when you are tempted to take drugs, supposedly to improve your performance. This book tells you what these drugs can do, what the rules say about them, how unscrupulous dealers make money from them, and why the drugs are harmful to the user and to sports.

❝ *The important thing in life is not the triumph but the struggle. The essential thing is not to have conquered but to have fought well.*
Baron Pierre de Coubertin, founder of the modern Olympics, in 1908. **❞**

WHY TAKE SPORTS DRUGS?

"I heard that my rival had started drugs. I thought, he's gonna win. Could I let him get away with it?"

Why should an athlete, a swimmer, a football player, a weightlifter, want to take a drug? These people are supposed to be at the peak of health and fitness. Why should they want to put something into their bodies designed to treat people who are ill? It seems to go against all logic.

It certainly goes against what sports are all about: playing a game or event, for the sake of taking part and enjoying it. If you play football, or swim, or run, or throw darts, you probably enjoy what you do. You probably also want to improve. You may wish to represent your school, college or club, or even your district, state or country. In some people, the desire to win is so strong that they inevitably come face to face with the dilemma of drugs. Should you take something that is supposed to help you do better?

"I feel I have to take drugs"

When sports people turn to drugs, they look for a drug that they believe will help them run faster or longer without getting exhausted. Or they may want a drug to make them feel more aggressive, or to help build up their muscles. Some sports affected by drug misuse do not involve too much physical activity, such as shooting or billiards. Players here may look for a drug that they believe will steady their nerves and reduce tension.

Hundreds of drugs have been used in these ways. It doesn't matter to some people if there is little evidence that

Physique, technique and determination make a top-class competitor.

a drug really does improve performance. They just believe firmly that this is what they need.

Some people have such a compulsive desire to win, at all costs, that they knowingly risk their lives. A physician asked 100 runners if they'd take a drug that would make them Olympic champions – but then would kill them within a year. Half of the runners said "Yes."

Sometimes people don't even realize what they are taking. When bodybuilders, weightlifters and similar competitors started misusing anabolic steroids in the 1950s no one really knew what might happen. It was like a medical experiment. Then the many risks became clear – liver cancer and stunted growth in teenagers, to name only two. Some bodybuilders stopped taking them. Yet others continued, thinking: "It can't happen to me." Of course, it can.

"Others do it, so why shouldn't I?"

A "need" from within yourself, an internal desire to take drugs, is one aspect. Maybe you aren't like that. Maybe you believe that only drug addicts – "junkies" – think in this way.

❝ *I heard that my rival had started drugs. I thought, he's gonna win. Could I let him get away with it?*
Weightlifter. ❞

But what happens when you find out that the winner of the last race or the last game, or the local champion or national hero, was misusing drugs?

If winning is so important to you, and others who win seem to be taking drugs — why not you? One mistake is to assume that they win because of the drugs. The fact is, some studies have found that it's the losers of the race who have been taking drugs. Basically, just taking a drug (a so-called "performance aid") isn't going to make you a champion.

Another mistake is to assume that you must follow the crowd, and do what they do. Many people who abuse drugs such as heroin and cocaine do it because of pressure from their friends. They find themselves unable to resist. Surely you don't think in this way, like a drug addict on the skids?

"Think of the money"

Professional players in dozens of sports, from football to billiards, can earn a small fortune if they win a championship. Just to get on to the "pro" team can mean a huge salary. But once you're there, you need to stay there. This can be another pressure to take drugs, to keep your job for another few years.

❝ If you're not on anything, it's like lining up on the blocks with trainers when everyone else is wearing spikes.
International sprinter ❞

But the longer a drug is taken, the higher the risks to health. Addiction is possible . . . what was it you thought about drug addicts?

In team sports, the money involved is not only important to an individual player. The coach, the manager, the people who own the team and make a profit from it – they are all involved. But they aren't the ones taking the drug, and the risks.

"Drugs are so available"
Some people say that if drugs were more difficult to get hold of, then there might be less temptation to use them. Unfortunately this is not so. Some people make money from

Having to avoid drugs is now a hurdle facing many athletes.

trading illegally in drugs, and they will always make sure drugs are available to pass around the locker room.

Once sports people reach a high level of competition, they will probably hear about drugs and where to get hold of them. Even in weight-training gyms and fitness clubs, or in high school sports, you may find drugs for sale. The very fact that drugs are there is enough to turn some "clean" athletes into drug users. Yet other drugs are available in many cities. They include heroin, crack, marijuana . . . shades of thinking like a junkie again?

> ❝ *One of my friends collapsed on the platform. His leg muscles had given out. We were both taking steroid drugs. I knew the same thing could happen to me.*
> **Weightlifter.** ❞

Turning down drugs

The best athletes, such as the American Carl Lewis, have always said "No" to drugs. They know the dangers and truly believe in fair competition. Champions such as Lewis and Britain's Sebastian Coe have succeeded by talent, hard work, the right attitude and regular training. They know the arguments against drugs. Taking a drug to help you win is cheating, it is potentially dangerous to your health, and it harms the name of sports.

> ❝ *She came in looking worried to death. She'd seen the doctor. Things had gone wrong. I never even knew she was on drugs.* ❞

DRUGS MISUSE IN SPORTS

"People are looking for short-cuts to being champions..."

Many different drugs are open to abuse by people involved in sports. Of course, athletes and other sports people are only human. Like us, occasionally they become ill and need medical treatment with a drug. The problems arise when they use them in the attempt to give an unfair advantage over competitors.

Drugs taken as so-called "performance aids" include:

- *stimulants that make you alert, "high" and wakeful*
- *anabolic steroids, that build up body muscle*
- *hormonal growth-promoters, that also encourage development of body tissues*
- *strong painkillers, most of which are illegal, because they are powerful and addictive*
- *beta-blockers (a type of heart drug), that calm and steady a player in a sport that needs careful co-ordination*
- *diuretics, that help dilute urine or reduce weight by removing water from the body.*

Many drugs are banned from various sports by the International Olympic Committee (IOC) and by the various controlling organizations for each sport in different countries. Some of their effects on the body are explained in this chapter – the ones that drug abusers believe will help them. The more important effects – the harmful ones – are explained in the next chapter.

Stimulants

Stimulants include a whole range of substances, from caffeine (found in tea and coffee) through amphetamines to cocaine. As the name suggests, they stimulate the body, mentally and physically.

These drugs may make you feel alert and bounding with energy. But when the effects wear off, you feel "down" and depressed. Some stimulants can make pain easier to bear, and they cause a surge in confidence and feeling "high." Often, people who take amphetamines believe they are doing better, when in fact their performance is worse. Amphetamines can also make some people feel more aggressive than usual.

Drugs related to amphetamine include dextroamphetamine and methamphetamine. They are sometimes called "speed," "uppers" or "pep pills."

❝❝ *I listened to his story about how he felt a great buzz and energy out of cocaine. That's what made me think, I could use a bit of that . . .* **❞❞**

Amphetamines were originally used medically to treat people with an illness called *narcolepsy*, in which there is an overwhelming desire to sleep. They were also taken by people who wanted to lose weight rapidly, because these types of drugs stop you feeling hungry. For many years they could be bought without a doctor's prescription. But they caused many problems, and nowadays they are strictly controlled in most countries.

Amphetamines work by releasing two natural chemicals, called adrenaline and nor-adrenaline, from their glands into the blood. These chemicals cause the muscles to tense, the heart to beat faster and the blood pressure to rise. Depending on how much you take they can make you feel awake, alert, unable to relax and constantly agitated, for hours or days. (Adrenaline is also known as epinephrine.)

❝ The judges looked at his eyes. That was the giveaway. ❞

Despite the laws, amphetamines are still misused. A few years ago, a sports doctor said he estimated 40 per cent of major-league baseball players used amphetamines. They are taken by people who believe the drug will enable them to keep going, past their natural exhaustion barrier. The "placebo effect" (page 23) often plays a part in such a belief.

Cocaine is also a habit-forming stimulant and has many similarities to amphetamines, except the "high" is much shorter — it usually lasts less than one hour. Cocaine has

Len Bias, US basketball star, whose death was linked to drug abuse.

become known as the "drug of the 80s" and it has certainly crept into sports in this decade. In the United States, between 15 and 20 million people are thought to have taken cocaine, including some of the nation's top sports stars. But it kills. Basketball star Len Bias died in 1986, from a heart attack supposedly triggered by cocaine.

Cocaine, like amphetamines, makes you numb to pain, so that a competitor could play fiercer and tackle harder. This explains why it has crept into sports such as football and ice hockey. There are also signs that cocaine abuse may be spreading to track events.

The other main group of stimulants belong to a type called sympathomimetic amines (SMAs). When these are taken in high doses they cause the blood vessels to widen and the heart to beat faster. Like amphetamines and

cocaine, they are banned from sports. But they are not illegal outside sports, and some of them can be bought in a drug store, without a prescription. This is because some SMAs (ephedrine, pseudoephedrine and phenylpropanolamine) are common ingredients in cold and hay-fever remedies. And they may be used to treat respiratory diseases, because they encourage the lungs and airways to open up.

Anabolic steroids

These are perhaps the most commonly abused drugs in sports (called "juice", "gear" or "roids"). They are used by athletes who want to build up body muscle, for weightlifting, shot-put and other sports that require explosive, short-term strength. They are used by some bodybuilders, too, and may be spreading to track events.

Anabolic means to "build up" or "construct". *Steroid* is the name given to one group of the natural body chemicals called hormones. Most anabolic steroids misused in sports are similar to the male hormone testosterone, a substance produced in the man's testes (testicles). There are around 120 different anabolic steroid preparations on sale throughout the world, going by names such as Dianabol, Durabolin, Winstrol and Anavar.

Anabolic steroids have a medical use for people with cancer, or those recovering from surgery that keeps them bed-bound.

When abused, anabolic steroids "inflate" the muscles.

The bodybuilder's bulges, attained by training, not chemicals.

The muscles look bigger, but the evidence is debatable that the drugs increase their strength. Anabolic steroids also have another effect, called the androgenic effect. This increases male bodily features: whiskers on the face, a deep voice and possibly more aggression. It happens in women as well as men.

Although people who take anabolic steroids say they become stronger on the drugs, there is no scientific evidence to support this claim. It may be that because anabolic steroids increase aggression and the competitive urge, this makes people train harder to build up strength. The "placebo" effect (see panel) may also be involved.

Shipianek of East Germany, suspended after misusing drugs.

The "placebo" effect

When doctors test a new drug, they give it to a group of volunteer patients. And to another, similar group, they give the "same" preparation – the same, that is, except for the actual drug itself. If one group gets pink syrup (with the drug), the other group also gets pink syrup (the placebo, without the drug). The patients do not know which group they are in.

This is done to avoid what's known as the "placebo effect." It is well known that simply taking something, like a pill or medicine, can make you believe it will make you well. This belief may be strong enough to make you well. So when doctors test their two groups of volunteers, both groups think they are getting the drug, and so both believe equally that it will work. This removes any bias.

Misusing drugs in sports can also involve the placebo effect. The takers believe that the drug will make them stronger, or more muscular, or give them extra stamina. The belief may work by spurring them on to train that bit harder, for instance.

Anabolic steroids have spread from weightlifting and "power" field events (shot, javelin, hammer, discus) to gyms and fitness clubs. They are also taken by non-competitive bodybuilders.

Unlike stimulant drugs, which are used at the event, anabolic steroids are treated as "training drugs." This means they are often taken for a long time in the training period before a competition. People may start off on one anabolic steroid and then add another, and another. In the end they may be taking 5 to 15 times the normal medical dose. Usually they come off the drugs a few weeks before the competition, to reduce the risk of being caught if they have a drug test.

Anabolic steroids have many harmful effects, particularly when misused for months or years at high doses. Some effects do not disappear when the drug is stopped. No one knows how many people abuse them. One authority on sports medicine estimates that 70 to 80 per cent of all anabolic steroids made are used against the rules by sports people.

❞❞ People are looking for short-cuts to being champions – and that's what taking steroids is all about: cheating, just downright cheating. ❞❞

In one American gym, almost half of 250 weightlifters had used anabolic steroids at some time. When 50 of these were questioned, 28 of them said they did not enter any competitions. They used anabolic steroids simply to improve their looks, their physique and "image." Of the 50, 12 had been using them for more than two or three years.

Hormonal growth-promoters
Anabolic steroids are one type of hormonal growth-promoter. In the last few years some athletes have started to use other natural hormones that encourage growth of certain body parts. One of these is growth hormone, a

substance that makes us all grow during childhood. This hormone would never normally be given to an adult, for medical reasons. Also, it is very expensive. Yet some athletes are paying for supplies of it because they think it will help them grow or develop more muscle.

Another hormone being abused is human chorionic gonadotrophin (HCG for short). It is only produced by pregnant women. But some male athletes are using it in much the same way as anabolic steroids, to try and build up muscle, because it stimulates the production of testosterone.

Strong painkillers

Everyone takes a painkiller now and again. An aspirin for a headache, or a paracetamol. However, the types of painkillers banned in sports are extremely strong, addictive types known as narcotic analgesics. They include heroin (diamorphine) and a related drug, morphine.

As explained above, some people believe that painkillers might encourage them to tackle harder and play on through injury. Sprays on the skin that temporarily deaden pain are one thing. But the narcotic analgesics are among the most addictive and dangerous drugs known, in sports or anywhere else.

Beta-blockers and diuretics

Some sports figures don't want to be stimulated or have bulging muscles. Snooker players, archers and shooters need to be calm and relaxed, with steady nerves.

Beta-blockers are drugs that slow down the heartbeat

Miscueing: some snooker players have been tempted to drugs.

> **❝ I suppose we thought there'd be no real harm.
> Just one go . . . but then another, and another.
> Just like a junkie. ❞**

rate and help control stress and panic. There are many different versions available. They are widely used by doctors to treat patients with certain types of heart disease and high blood pressure. Beta-blockers are banned by the IOC because they could give people an advantage in certain sports. The IOC says that there are alternative drugs for people who have heart problems.

These drugs would not be used by athletes or other

people involved in a sport that demands speed and endurance. For this reason the International Amateur Athletic Federation (IAAF) does not ban or test for beta-blockers. The IOC only tests for them in sports where physical activity is of little importance.

The World Professional Billiards and Snooker Association agrees that beta-blockers should be banned. Certain players have admitted to taking them in recent times.

Some players say that they need these drugs for an illness. And they point out that taking a beta-blocker would have much the same effect on nerves as a couple of bottles or cans of beer, and beer is not banned as such. The risks in taking beta-blockers are described on page 35.

❛❛ *Today, 16-year-olds are making lifts that, 15 years ago, grown men were unable to achieve. Don't tell me that school milk has made all that difference.* **❜❜**
Member of the British Amateur Weightlifting Association.

Diuretics are also on the IOC's list of banned drugs. They remove fluids from the body, and are prescribed medically for certain heart and kidney complaints. In sports, they have been used by some people who want to lose weight before an event (in boxing, wrestling and other sports that involve weight categories, for example). Sometimes they are taken to get rid of fluids, to make other misused drugs more difficult to detect.

Blood doping

Blood doping ("boosting" or "blood packing") does not involve drugs, but it is an unfair method of getting an advantage in sports that call for endurance.

A doctor takes a pint or two of blood from the athlete about two months before the competition. This blood is frozen. About two days before the competiton, the red cells from the frozen blood are given back to the athlete by an injection. (Red cells carry oxygen to the muscles and other tissues.) In the meantime, though, the athlete's body has made more red cells, to replace those taken away. So there are now many more red cells than usual. This "extra-rich" blood can carry more oxygen to the muscles, and thus helps in sports that call for stamina. This procedure has been used by skiers, marathon racers and weightlifters.

When is a drug not a drug?

Many drugs that are used to treat genuine illnesses are not banned from sports – because they could not give a competitor any advantage. Antibiotics, taken for infections, are an example.

But what about "everyday" drugs, such as the stimulant caffeine? This is found naturally in cups of tea and coffee, cola drinks and chocolate bars. According to the IOC, yes, caffeine is a stimulant drug and so is banned. But the ban only applies to large quantities of caffeine. You would have to drink well over 10 cups of strong coffee quickly, or eat several family-sized bars of chocolate in one go, to risk breaking the limit.

THE HARM IN DRUGS

"Playing with needles? No way, not with AIDS looking over my shoulder."

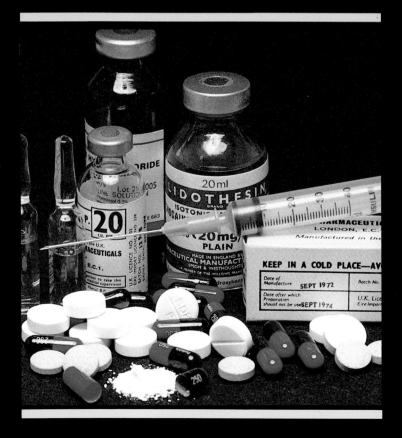

Taking any drug involves risk. When drugs are used to treat illness, the doctor assesses the risks and decides whether they are outweighed by the benefits. When drugs are taken by a fit and healthy person, that person is taking the risks but not receiving the intended benefits.

All the drugs that sports people misuse have harmful effects. Some are worse than others. Almost always, the risks increase when drugs are used in high doses and over a long time.

Stimulants

One of the main problems with stimulants, such as amphetamines, is that they can speed you up too much. This over-stimulation makes your heart race and you feel dizzy and restless. In large doses the drugs can over-ride the body's normal feeling of exhaustion. This feeling is natural and sensible, since it stops the body from going "over the top" and damaging itself. But in athletics and cycling, amphetamines have caused people to collapse because they pushed themselves too far. In the 1960 Olympics a Danish cyclist, Knud Jensen, collapsed and died after taking amphetamines.

Other dangers of amphetamines include the aggressive feelings they bring out in some people, and surges in blood pressure that may lead to collapse and death. There is also the important problem of addiction, in this case "psychological" addiction, where the mind needs the drug more than the body. For example, some people who come off amphetamines feel hopelessly low and depressed. This makes them more likely to go back to the drugs again, in order to get high and feel the sense of elation and confidence.

Cocaine can be very damaging, especially if it is used for a long time and regularly. "Snorting" the drug through the nose can soon cause nosebleeds and sores. It may even "burn" a hole through the membrane that separates the two nostrils. The risks of having a heart attack may increase as cocaine disturbs the normal rhythm of the heart. This could be extremely dangerous in a competitor exerting hard physically. It might lead to collapse.

❝ On the day, in the heat of the moment, you don't really care about risks. You gotta win, so you take it. ❞

Even the types of stimulants found in cold and hay-fever remedies can be dangerous when taken by athletes competing in an event. These drugs can make the blood vessels become narrowed and change the rhythm of the heart – again, extremely dangerous to someone running hard.

Strong painkillers

Narcotic analgesics are banned not only in sports. They are tightly-controlled drugs in most Western countries. Possession can lead to fines or imprisonment if wrongly used, or used at all. This is partly due to the great risk of addiction and to stop dealing.

There is another reason to ban strong painkillers from

Birgit Dressel, who abused drugs and later died.

sport. They may make someone who is already injured push far beyond the normal pain barrier. These athletes may find themselves severely and permanently injured as a result.

> **It's no good trying to scare them by saying their balls will drop off.**
> **BBC TV commentator and coach.**

Anabolic steroids and growth hormones

More and more harmful effects of anabolic steroids have come to light over the years. For a long time people realized the obviously harmful effects in women who took them.

They developed deep voices and facial hair – and they did not go back to normal when they stopped the drugs. A West German, Birgit Dressel, was a heptathlete who came fourth in the 1986 European Athletics Championships. She died later and was found to have been taking a cocktail of two different anabolic steroids (as well as other drugs).

Young people who take anabolic steroids may stop growing altogether. Adult men who take them are also at risk. A 26-year-old bodybuilder, who had taken a mixture of five different anabolic steroids for four years, died in hospital of liver cancer. Two other athletes died of kidney cancer after taking them.

Anabolic steroids can affect the mind and make people aggressive and potentially dangerous. One steroid-user in Boston, Massachusetts, became uncontrollably angry when another car driver "cut him off" on the street. He got out and smashed the other car's window with a crowbar.

Doctors now believe that people who take anabolic steroids for many years are more likely to die from heart attacks. This is because the drugs change the levels of fats in the blood, and fats are linked to heart attacks.

No one knows exactly what damage growth hormone may do to the adult body. It may cause the bones to thicken, especially in the hands, feet and jaw. This is what happens to a few people who have *acromegaly*, an illness in which the body naturally produces too much growth hormone.

Tina Plakinger, bodybuilder, beat her steroid habit.

'I WAS TURNING INTO A MAN'

'I threw my husband against the door and hit him again and again'

Beta-blockers and diuretics

Beta-blockers slow the beating rate of the heart. This could be dangerous if the taker already has a slow heartbeat – as many very fit people do. These drugs can also cause a side-effect known as *bronchospasm*, where the airways leading to the lungs tighten and make it difficult to breathe.

Diuretics work by removing water from the body. They can cause serious dehydration (drying-out of body tissues) in athletes who take them. They can also cause blood disorders, rashes, and stomach upsets in some people.

❝ *Not only did we have to pay through the nose for the drug, the needle cost the earth, too.* ❞

Blood doping

Blood doping is a risky procedure, especially if the blood donated to the athlete before a race is from someone else. Such blood may contain the microbes that cause diseases like hepatitis and AIDS. Because the blood is given back to the athlete through a needle, there is the added danger of infections from needles that are not perfectly sterile.

There is also the strong possibility that an athlete who races with boosted blood may push too hard and strain the heart, or the body may react against the extra cells.

Other dangers in illegal drugs

Often, with illegal drugs, the powder, tablet or solution that contains the drug is not pure. It has not been made under proper medical supervision, in clean laboratory conditions. It may contain impurities, some of which are highly dangerous.

Athletes have taken anabolic steroids made, not for legal medical use in humans, but for use in animals, to produce extra-lean meat. Bottles and packages of drugs have had their "*For veterinary use only*" labels removed and "*For human use*" labels put in their place, by crooked dealers. Drugs intended for animals may be more dangerous because they are usually not so pure and their strength is less carefully measured.

There are also dangers in how the drug is taken. Some anabolic steroids are taken by injection. This immediately puts the user at risk of diseases such as AIDS and hepatitis, if he or she is not careful about using new, perfectly sterile needles and syringes each time. An American weightlifter developed AIDS after sharing needles for injecting anabolic steroids with fellow bodybuilders. AIDS is incurable. He was, literally, "dying to win."

❝ *Playing with needles? No way, not with AIDS looking over my shoulder.* **❞**

RUG TESTIN

AND

THE RULES

"When I saw my name on the list, I almost fainted"

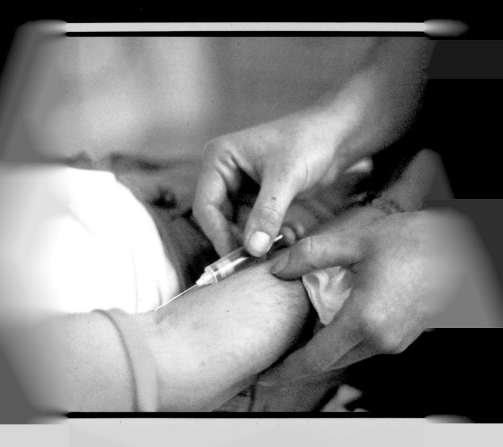

If you misuse drugs, you not only blemish the name of sports and risk your health, you also risk being suspended or banned from competitions, and having your prizes, medals and records taken away. Civil penalties for some drugs, such as cocaine, heroin and amphetamines, may be a heavy fine or prison.

Many different classes of drugs have been banned from sports by the IOC, which governs the Olympic Games. National and international bodies governing different sports, such as the International Amateur Athletic Federation (IAAF), also have lists of banned drugs. In amateur sports most governing bodies follow the IOC rules, perhaps changing them slightly, but still applying them to all members of the governing body in that sport.

Independent analysis at approved labs detects drug misusers.

But how do they know when someone has taken a certain drug? Drug controls only became possible when drug tests were developed. In a sense, the rules can only be as strict as the tests allow.

IOC banned drugs

The International Olympic Committee has strict rules on which drugs cannot be used by competitors. (Rarely there may be a medical reason for a competitor taking such a drug.) The list includes:

All stimulants, including caffeine in high quantities, cocaine and amphetamines

Narcotic analgesics (painkillers) such as heroin, morphine, pethidine and codeine

Anabolic steroids, testosterone and growth hormones

Beta-blockers and diuretics

Blood doping techniques

The IOC also banned all "pharmacological, physical and chemical manipulations" from the 1988 Olympic Games in Seoul. This means it can disqualify people who try to cheat the testing system by taking a drug that is not banned, in order to disguise the presence of one that is banned.

The development of drug tests

The first time competitors were tested for drug misuse at the Olympic Games was in 1968, at the Winter Olympics in Grenoble. Thorough testing began at the Munich Games in 1972. Since then, testing has been done at all Olympic Games and all major international events.

The test for anabolic steroids was developed in 1973. It helped to bring steroid use in international events under some control. However since then, athletes have tried to avoid detection in various ways.

What about substances like the hormone testosterone, which is found naturally in a man's body? Scientists have got around this by measuring the amount of testosterone compared to another naturally produced hormone, epitestosterone. They do the test on urine samples. Men who had very high levels of testosterone, compared to epitestosterone, are known to have taken this extra testosterone illegally.

What does testing involve?

Scientists can now detect many different drugs by testing a sample of urine. When a drug is taken, some of it may pass into the urine. Or the drug is broken down into different substances, and these also eventually find their way into the

❝ *When I saw my name on the list, I almost fainted. I thought it would never happen to me.* ❞

urine. Drug tests therefore look for the presence of the drug itself or its breakdown products, called *metabolites*.

The equipment used to test urine samples is complex and expensive, but extremely sensitive and accurate. Two scientific techniques are used: gas chromatography and mass spectrometry. The results from these tests give a "fingerprint" of all the substances that a person has taken, days or sometimes weeks before the urine sample is given.

When a person is chosen to be tested, there is no way out. Refusal is taken as meaning "guilty."

For the test, the person is asked to urinate into a large beaker. The sample is divided into two and both parts are sealed in bottles and sent to an approved independent laboratory. Only one bottle is tested at first. If the test indicates a banned substance is present, the governing body of the sport is informed. The second sample is then tested with qualified observers present if necessary.

❝ James didn't realize the rules had changed. Lucky one of us caught him, before the officials.❞

Dozens of competitors are tested at a large sporting event. But testing at events does little to curb drug use out of season, and during training. And sports participants have tried various tricks to avoid detection of drug misuse. Some athletes have taken a drug called probenecid, which is used legally to treat gout. It has a side-effect of stopping anabolic steroids from seeping into the urine. However, probenecid itself shows up on the new tests which are being introduced.

There have also been accusations of cheating, when the urine samples are collected. Some athletes say that it is easy to switch bottles or to bribe an official to swap the athlete's "dirty" sample of urine for a "clean" one before it is tested.

Who can be tested?

In the Olympic Games and at most major international championships, the first three in each event are tested at the end of that event. This approach of testing winners is used in many national events, too.

Testing for drugs does not just apply to adults. Children of school age have been tested in badminton, cyclecross, athletics, judo, skating, weightlifting and swimming. For those under 16 years of age, most sports organizations insist that parents are involved and give their consent.

In 1986, IOC-approved laboratories around the world carried out over 32,000 tests. Positive results were:

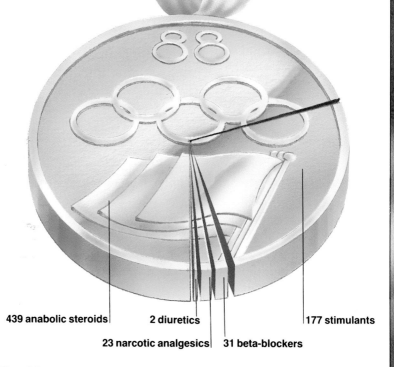

439 anabolic steroids | 2 diuretics | 177 stimulants

23 narcotic analgesics | 31 beta-blockers

Finn Martti Vainio (right) lost his 1984 Olympic silver for steroids.

Random testing

"Random testing" means players can be asked to give a urine sample whether they win or not. It is becoming more common at national standard in many sports. Athletes are selected at random just before an event takes place and informed after the event, given a form to sign, and asked to go to the testing station within a certain time. If they refuse, they are treated as having a positive result.

Several countries and sports are trying to introduce random testing during training sessions. In other words, competitors can be tested at any time in the sport's season, not just at an event. This may be the only way that drug misuse can be stamped out. Britain's Sports Council oversees all amateur sports and advises governing bodies of sport on drug control. It is introducing random drug tests, out of season as well as at competitions. It wants to introduce this system to all sports in the UK.

The IAAF, which governs athletics worldwide, has agreed in principle to random testing throughout the year. But the costs of such tests would be huge. It could be several years before the IAAF works out a way of doing this evenly across all its member countries, which include Western and Eastern nations.

Testing in different countries

In the United States, testing is carried out at many national, state and regional amateur events.

In professional sports, such as baseball and football, testing is very much down to the professional association of

In professional sport, rules should be as tough as players.

the sport involved. The rules vary considerably, from one sport to another, and from one country to another.

In Britain, professional soccer players have been tested since 1979. Rugby League began testing players in 1986. In the United States, the National Basketball Association introduced testing in 1983. Professional baseball players became subject to drugs tests in 1986. The first testing of tennis players was in 1986, at Wimbledon and the US Open.

In France, Belgium and Greece, national laws have been passed to ban the use of drugs in sport, with heavy penalties. In most other countries, misusing drugs in sports is not actually against the law of the land, unless the drug itself is illegal.

What happens if you have a positive test?

In the United States and Britain, if a competitor has a positive drug test, then what happens next is usually decided by the governing body of the sport. One British Amateur Athletic Club, decided to ban for life any of its members found using drugs.

Many people argue that the "punishments" imposed by some clubs and governing bodies are not harsh enough. Some athletes who have had a positive drug test have been shielded by their governing body, which has refused to name them. In Britain this will undoubtedly change, as the Sports Council begins to insist on naming athletes who have taken drugs. The Sports Council recommends that people who have a positive drug test should be banned from recognized competitions in their sport – for life.

The IOC says that athletes found to have taken steroids, narcotics, amphetamines and certain other drugs should be banned from competitions for three years. If they are caught again, the ban should be for life. For "accidentally" taking the more everyday drugs such as ephedrine and codeine, there should be a three-month ban for the first offence, two years for the second, and a life ban for the third.

❝ *I was amazed when they called our son for a test ... I thought it only happened at the Olympics and big-money meetings.* ❞

THE TRADE IN SPORTS DRUGS

"I heard a joke that the weightlifters had trouble carrying their suitcases, they were so full of drugs..."

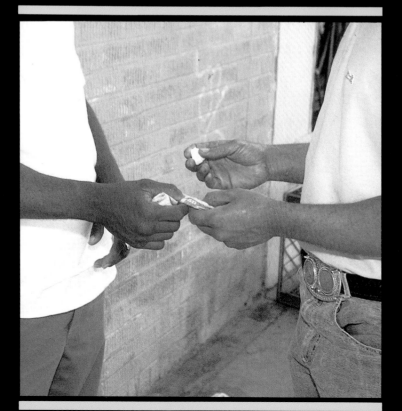

Many of the drugs banned from sports have uses in everyday medicine. Doctors prescribe anabolic steroids occasionally, and beta-blockers and diuretics are used by thousands of patients who have heart disease or high blood pressure. For some drugs, it is possible for athletes to get hold of a supply by bringing pressure on a doctor in some way, to provide a prescription or certificate.

Medicine itself controls drugs strictly. In Britain the 1971 Misuse of Drugs Act makes it a punishable offense to sell, possess, import or dispense drugs such as amphetamines, cocaine and heroin, without a special certificate. The same types of laws apply in many other parts of the world.

But dealers in illegal drugs do not find this a problem, as we know from the rising levels of drug abuse among people in general. Amphetamines can easily be bought in many major cities. The drugs are often made in secret "factories" and smuggled across international borders every day. The distribution network for sports drugs is much the same as for cocaine, heroin and marijuana: a series of dealers, traffickers and pushers, who each take a share of the vast profits made from supplying illicit drugs.

I got them from the doctor

Anabolic steroids are easier to get hold of than amphetamines in most countries. Ordinary doctors can write a prescription for these drugs and it is not illegal for pharmacists to dispense them. Many people claim that it is not difficult (especially in the United States) to persuade a doctor somehow to give them anabolic steroids for sport. A few doctors will dish out enough drugs for an entire baseball team. When athletes are asked where they get their supplies from, about 1 in 3 say: "From a physician." In some countries anabolic steroids can even be bought directly from a drugstore, without a doctor's prescription.

It is estimated that American athletes spend nearly $100 million a year on anabolic steroids. Most are bought through black-market channels. These channels involve unscrupulous health professionals and also people involved in legitimate drug distribution, such as drug wholesalers. Major drug dealers may even advertise their products by direct mail and send out catalogues and price lists. A book, the *Underground Steroid Handbook*, keeps buyers up-to-date

Rules vary between countries on which drugs need prescriptions.

on new drugs, black market prices, and even on ways to beat drug detection. Advertisements for special "vitamin preparations" appear in some magazines, like those bought by bodybuilders. In fact, what you may get is an injectable drug, complete with syringe and needle.

Sport's underground network

Sometimes the supply of drugs for an athlete may come via a coach or team physician, or from a teammate. In some areas anabolic steroids are sold by shady dealers in gyms and fitness clubs.

At the top levels of sports, it is clear there are sophisticated drug rings. Sometimes the rings involve competitors themselves, who smuggle drugs from countries where there are few controls. One weightlifter, returning from a trip to Rumania, apparently brought into the United

❝ Unless something is done soon, international sport will be a competition between circus freaks manipulated by international chemists. ❞

States 1,600 tablets of Nerobol (an anabolic steroid).

In some countries (like Britain) it is not illegal to possess certain drugs, such as anabolic steroids. But it is against the law to sell them to other people. At the moment people can legally import a drug such as an anabolic steroid, for their own use and on prescription.

David Jenkins (far right) admitted involvement in drug trading.

In 1986-7, United States investigators broke a massive drugs ring, said to have supplied about two-thirds of all anabolic steroids taken by American athletes. Britain's Olympic medal-winning sprinter, David Jenkins, was one of those charged with heading the drug ring. People involved in the ring smuggled tons of drugs from Mexico into the United States, and sold them to athletes and coaches at a vast profit. The drugs were smuggled in concealed compartments in various motor vehicles or concealed in plastic pouches strapped to the smugglers' legs.

> ❛❛ *I heard a joke that the weightlifters had trouble carrying their suitcases, they were so full of drugs . . .* ❜❜

WINNING WITHOUT DRUGS

❝ At the presentation, that's when I felt so proud. I'd done it without pills and potions. I'd really shown them. ❞

You do not need to take drugs to have fun in sports. You do not need them to make you a winner – whether local champion, national star or Olympic gold medalist. In almost all cases the people who take drugs are the losers, in all senses of the word.

Doing well in your sport, enjoying it, and winning if that is really important to you – it all comes down to regular training, often very hard work, a good diet and the right attitude.

Attitude counts. Most people who take part in a sport want to get better at it, to improve. You may want to get into your school team or represent the local club. Perhaps your aims are higher. But take time out to decide how much you can put into your sport and what you want from it.

It is a good idea to sit back occasionally and think about how you are getting on in your sport, whether or not you are achieving what you want. Set some sort of goal for yourself, but make it realistic.

The importance of training

Improving at sports usually involves a training program. This is probably best worked out with a coach or teacher. Expert advice and help is vital. You may need to develop speed, endurance, alertness, suppleness or strength, all to different degrees.

Simply playing your sport, be it basketball, soccer, swimming or whatever, helps you improve. But if you are

World-beater Carl Lewis has spoken out many times against drugs.

serious, you will want to work on a training schedule. Perhaps you will want to run to build up your stamina and general fitness, and weight-train to build up muscle strength. It depends on what your sport calls for.

When it comes to technical skill, you'll probably find it helpful to watch those who are already experts in your sport. Study videos or read books, and once again, a good teacher or coach is vital.

However keen and impatient you are to improve, you should never train so hard that you always feel exhausted. Knowing when to stop and relax for a while is just as important as training, if you want to keep on top form.

The right start: good coaching and a sensible training program.

Eating the right food

You'll soon find that what you eat can have a big effect on how well you compete. Many training programs include advice on what you should eat, both when training and when competing in an event.

For example, if your interest is a strength sport then a high-protein diet, with plenty of meat and fish, will be needed. Long-distance runners eat lots of starchy foods such as potatoes, bread or rice. After training or competing, remember that you have probably sweated and lost a lot of your body's water. You may need to drink water or juices to replace it.

In the end . . .

Taking drugs as a short-cut to skill, training and the right attitude will never pay off. There's so much more to doing well in sports than using drugs. And there is a lot more to sports than simply winning.

One day, the coach called me in and said I'd probably never make it to the top level. She was right. I'd never even considered it.

DRUG PROFILES

Stimulants

Examples	Benzedrine (speed), ephedrine, cocaine, and benzamphet-amine
Main effects	Increase alertness, reduce tiredness, increase heart beat, give feelings of elation and confidence. May also make you feel more aggressive and competitive. May reduce appetite and make you feel irritable and restless.
Addictiveness	Some stimulant drugs are psychologically addictive. Some people want to take more and more, to maintain the high .
Ways of taking	Most stimulants are taken as tablets. Cocaine may be inhaled as a powder through the nose ("snorting") or inhaled as fumes.
Harmful effects	Cocaine and amphetamines are the most harmful drugs in this class. They can cause heart palpitations, sweating and raised blood pressure. In overdose you may collapse, suffer convulsions and die.
Medical uses	Amphetamines and cocaine are now rarely used medically. Amphetamines have been used in the past as appetite suppressants ("diet pills") and to treat severe depression. Ephedrine and related chemicals are sometimes found in common cold remedies and medicines for hay fever, asthma and other respiratory diseases.

Anabolic steroids

Examples	Nandrolone, stanozolol fluoxymesterone, testosterone, oxandrolone, norethandrolone.
Main effects	Possibly increased muscle weight and size if taken with high-protein diet. They may cause virilization (development of male characteristics in boys and women, and also aggressiveness and competitiveness. Muscle size increases with prolonged use, but scientific studies are lacking on whether they increase strength.
Addictiveness	Anabolic steroids are not addictive in the true sense, but many people who use them find it difficult to stop taking them and see their bodies reduce.
Harmful effects	The risks of taking anabolic steroids over any length of time are enormous. In boys and young men they can stunt growth. In women they cause growth of facial hair, deeper voice and menstrual problems (may be irreversible.) In men steroids may liver cancer and

	may increase the risk of heart disease.
Medical uses	The many side-effects of anabolic steroids make them of limited use in medicine, although they are sometimes used for cancer patients who lose weight rapidly and for convalescent patients who have been unable to move from bed for a long time.

Narcotic analgesics

Examples	Heroin (diamorphine), morphine, methadone, pethidine, codeine.
Main effects	They act on the brain and nervous system so they are powerful painkillers. Some, such as heroin, are also misused as "recreational" drugs. May cause temporary feelings of pleasure or calm.
Addictiveness	Heroin is one of the most addictive drugs known, both mentally and physically. All narcotic analgesics carry some risk of addiction.
Harmful effects	Apart from addiction, narcotics can cause breathing problems and death. May cause dizziness, drowsiness, stomach ache, vomiting and constipation.
Medical uses	Narcotics such as morphine are sometimes used to relieve severe pain, for example in cancer

patients. Codeine is present in many over-the-counter preparations, which do not need a prescription, for mild pain relief.

Other drugs

Beta-blockers	Drugs normally used to treat heart disease, including atenolol, propranolol and oxpranolol.
Main effects	Slow down the heart beat and steady shaking hands. The risks are excessive slowing of the heart, heart failure and bronchospasm (sudden tightening of the airways to the lungs).
Diuretics	Drugs normally used to treat heart disease or high blood pressure by removing water from the body. They include bendroflumethiazide, furosemide and spironolactone.
Main effects	Diuretics take fluids out of the body and are used in some medical conditions where this is necessary, for example in high blood pressure. They can cause a rapid reduction in weight. The risks are stomach problems, drowsiness, rashes and blood disorders.

Blood doping

Blood doping means replacing some of a person's blood with concentrated red cells (the part of the blood that carries oxygen to the tissues), one or two days before an event. The red cells may have come from that person (taken out about two months before the event) or from another person see page 28.

Main effects	After blood doping, the athlete can carry more oxygen than normal to the muscles. This helps him or her run faster and longer before exhaustion.
Risks	The main risks occur when red cells from another person are given. The athlete may develop a rash or a fever, and there may be kidney damage if the wrong blood is used. There is also the risk of transmitting diseases such as hepatitis and AIDS.
Testing	Sports bodies, including the IOC, do not test for blood doping because of ethical problems. Any test would demand that a sample of blood be taken from the person at various stages before and after an event.

SOURCES OF HELP

Listed below are some organizations which should provide you with further information or printed matter.

The Challenge Program
United States Department of Education
Reporter's Building
7th and D Streets
Washington
D.C. 20202

Athletic Commission of New York Sta
270 Broadway
New York
New York 10007

American College of Sports Medicine
P.O. Box 1440
Indianapolis
Indiana 46206

United States Olympic Committee
1750 East Boulder Street
Colorado Springs
Colorado 80909

The Athletic Congress
5 West 63rd Street
New York
New York 10023

National Institute on Drug Abuse
5600 Fishers Lane
Rockville
Maryland 20857

National Council on Drug Abuse
571 West Jackson Avenue
Chicago
Illinois 60606

Public Affairs Pamphlets
381 Park Avenue South
New York
New York 10016

ational Hockey League
ublic Relations Department,
650 Fifth Avenue,
33rd Floor,
New York,
New York 10019

ational Clearinghouse for
rug Abuse Information
'.O. Box 416,
'ensington,
laryland 20795

ational Basketball Association
'Don't Foul Out",
'45 Fifth Avenue
lew York,
lew York 10022

epartment of Justice
Drug Enforcement Administration,
Vashington D.C. Division,
00 6th Street S.W.
Vashington,
D.C. 20024

rug Abuse Council, Inc.
'828 L Street N.W.,
Vashington,
D.C. 20036

ternational Amateur Athletic
ederation
IAFF, 3 Hans Crescent, London SW1
Telephone London (01) 581 8771
he IAFF is the international governing
ody of athletics and has 180 member
ederations around the world. It produces
s own list of *Doping Control Regulations*
nd distributes an anti-doping campaign
ooklet for young athletes, by the
ternational Athletic Foundation.

WHAT THE WORDS MEAN

amateur someone who participates in sport for fun or recognition or to keep fit – but not for money

anabolic something that helps to build up, develop or make bigger

analgesic drug that stops or reduces pain (a painkiller)

doping taking substances (drugs) in sport with the intention of gaining an unfair advantage over competitors

drug any substance that changes the body's workings (including the way the person's mind works, behaviour, etc.)

drug abuse non-medical drug use with harmful effects, on the abuser and possibly on others

governing body organization that is responsible for a sport, produces rules and arranges recognized competitions

hormone a natural chemical substance produced by the body which can affect the way it develops and works

narcotic analgesics painkillers related to morphine, which are highly addictive

professional someone who does something for money

steroid a substance with a particular type of chemical structure; several of the body's hormones are steroids, as are some drugs

stimulant a drug that stimulates the body's nervous system, especially the brain, to give feelings of increased alertness, physical and mental strength and energy

INDEX

acromegaly 34
addiction 11, 30
adrenaline 18
aggression 34
AIDS 29, 35
amphetamines 17, 48
anabolic steroids 10, 21, 32, 58
antibiotics 28

banned drugs 39
beta-blockers 25, 35, 59
Bias, Len 19
blood doping 28, 35, 59
British Amateur Weightlifting Association 27
bronchospasm 35

caffeine 18, 31
cancer 33
cocaine 18, 31
Coe, Sebastian 14

de Coubertin, Baron Pierre 6
dextroamphetamines 17
diuretics 27, 35, 58
Dressel, Birgit 32
drugs 5
   effects 17
   harm 30
   availability 12, 48

growth hormone 25, 34

HCG 25
heart attacks 34
hepatitis 35

International Amateur Athletic Association 27, 38, 44
International Olympic Committee 38, 46

Jenkins, David 50
Jenson, Knud 30

Lewis, Carl 14, 54

methamphetamine 17
Misuse of Drugs Act 48

narcotic analgesics 31, 59
National Basketball Association 45
national laws 44
noradrenaline 18

Olympic Games 39, 42

painkillers 25, 31
performance aids 11, 16
placebo effect 18, 23
Plakinger, Tina 34
probenecid 41
punishments 46

random testing 44
Rugby League 45

Shipianek 22
SMAs 19
Sports Council 5, 44, 46
steroids 21, 32, 58
stimulants 17, 30, 58

testing for drugs
   development 39
   what it involves 40
   who is tested 42
testosterone 21, 25
trade in drugs 48
training drugs 23

urine tests 40

Vainio, Martti 43

World Professional Billiards and Snooker Association 27

Photographic Credits:
Cover: Robert Harding; pages 4, 32-33 and 49: Robert Harding Library; pages 6, 20, 26, 37, 38, 53 and 55: Rex Features; pages 9, 12-13, 15, 45, 47 and 56: Frank Spooner Agency; page 19: Associated Press; pages 22 and 51: Colorsport; page 34: News of the World.

PRINTED IN BELGIUM BY

proost
INTERNATIONAL BOOK PRODUCTION